meet me here

——————————————————→

for the mother who holds so much

*"It may not be what you expected —
but it might just be what you needed."*

for my mother
who never slowed down enough to be seen —
but I saw you, always.
you gave so much of yourself,
and I hope this space gives a little piece of that back to you.

and to my 3 little cubs
thank you for letting me grow with you.
you've seen me in both the beauty and the breaking —
and still, you love me. I only hope you felt it too —
how deeply, how endlessly, I love you back.

Meet Me Here is a conversation-led journal that
weaves real-life storytelling with space for your own.
Created for the woman who holds so much,
this companion offers soft structure, emotional depth,
and a quiet place to land —
especially when you may need it most.

Each entry begins with a personal story —
sometimes mine, always yours.
You're invited to notice what rises:
connection, release, or simply a moment of recognition.

You don't have to have it all figured out to be here.
You just have to come as you are.

That's more than enough.
That's where we'll begin.

First edition, 2025
ISBN: 979-8-9987276-0-3
For permissions or inquiries,
please contact: meetmehere.co@gmail.com

contents

a letter from me to you

I can't handle small talk these days.

I know it has its place — how it keeps things friendly or even offers a bit of connection. But lately? My brain feels foggy. My emotions are stretched thin. And whatever energy I do have left... I need to protect it.

If you're here, I don't think I need to explain what that feels like. You probably know what it's like to carry a lot — to hold it all together with a blend of care and hidden exhaustion. To feel like you've disappeared inside a life you may also *deeply love*.

That's why I created this space.

If I'm being honest, I hesitate to even call this a *journal*. It's not quite a guided journal. Not quite a workbook. And it's not exactly a memoir — though I do share pieces of my story here. What I wanted most was to make something that felt like a conversation. Not the surface kind — but the kind held together by honesty, presence, and grace.

The stories I share come from a place of vulnerability. From the messy middle. Not because I have answers — but because I hope it makes you feel a little more seen — and maybe, safe enough to want to share, too. We may not walk the same paths in motherhood, in life even. But I believe when we speak openly, intentionally — we start to see just how much we hold in common.

And if you're here, walking alongside motherhood — as a daughter, a friend, a caregiver, or simply carrying an invisible load of your own — I hope you find some comfort here, too.

This isn't a journal that's meant to change you or push you toward some shinier version of yourself. It's a space to gently lay down all the things you've been holding on your own.

You don't have to fill every page. You can linger where something resonates. You can skip what doesn't. Or simply sit with the stories I've shared and see what stirs in you.

There's no wrong way to move through these pages — only your way.
All I ask is that you show up. Not for me, but for you.

So whenever you're ready, I'll be here — waiting to meet you.

With grace (not perfection),

Angelina

P.S. Just so you know — your love for your child is never in question here. That's already a given. You can feel frustrated in motherhood and still love your child more than life. Trust me — I get it. *And I got you.*

part i: the woman within

reconnecting with who you are beneath the role
through reflection, memory, and inner truth

before i knew better

I've always been good with kids. The fun aunt. The helper. The one who showed up for birthday parties, remembered every little detail, and somehow knew how to calm a crying toddler or connect with a too-cool-for-school preteen. People used to tell me I was "meant to be a mom." And honestly? I believed them. So when the time finally came, I really believed I was walking into it with intention.

We waited until we felt "ready" — the kind of ready where you've done the work, asked the questions, and set the plan. I prepared. I prayed. And because we decided to go the adoption route, I also researched as much as I could. I was determined to be the very best mom I could possibly be for my little boy.

My son was a toddler by the time we got the call to fly to Korea to meet him. He had already lived an entire lifetime before ever meeting us in person. For nearly two years, I watched him grow through photos and spent countless nights, imagining what our first encounter would be like. Would he call me *umma? Mommy* was out of the question — he didn't even speak English yet. But *umma...* a word I call my own mom, and what my mom called hers, felt natural. I had whispered it into photos, sending care packages with snapshots of our life to him on the other side of the world. Surely, that would mean something, right? Or would I be a complete stranger? I kept reminding myself not to have any expectations. But I couldn't help but hold on to the hope that he would be just as excited to see me as I was him.

When the time finally came, I couldn't believe it when he was right in front of me. It was surreal, to say the least. But as I stood there, staring intently and taking in the rush of emotions, my little boy — my son — said something that stopped my heart cold. When I heard his voice for the very first time, it wasn't *umma*, like I had imagined. Instead, he locked eyes with me and said something that would forever be etched into my memory: *Shibal.*

In that instant, I almost wished I didn't understand Korean. I even questioned if I had heard him right. After all, I was born in the States, so my level of understanding isn't nearly as good as my husband's, who was born in Korea. I looked over at him to see if I misunderstood and noticed that he acted like nothing happened. That was enough proof for me that I misheard our son and I happily moved on. But just as I started to feel at ease, he said it again — this time clear as day — and suddenly every ounce of my Korean comprehension came crashing down into one undeniable translation: *F*ck.*

Yes, that's right. While other moms get to nostalgically recall "Mama" as their baby's first word... mine — technically, was *f*ck.* I immediately froze. Not because I was offended, but because I suddenly realized: *I had no idea what I was doing.*

From the very first day I became a mother... I felt like I'd already failed. And since then, there have been so many more times when I still feel the same. Failure after failure. Defeat after defeat. I had imagined myself being the kind of mom who packed cute lunches and had picnics at the park. But instead, I became the opposite. You know — the one people quietly judge so they can feel a little better about themselves. Yep, that's me.

But after many meltdowns and tears (mine, not my children's) — I've come to learn something no one tells us enough: The version of motherhood we're shown, the one we're expected to live up to, is rarely the one we actually live. It's not about doing it all, or doing it well. It's about connecting. Meeting your kids where they are — in the good and the hard times. And knowing that trying your best is far more valuable than doing it perfectly.

I still have to remind myself every day that I'm a good mother, even when I don't fully believe it. It's hard to give yourself grace when you're in the thick of it, especially when motherhood looks nothing like you pictured. But the truth is, not one person walks into this fully ready.

And yet... the mother you are, the woman you are... still shows up. Quietly. Boldly. Unexpectedly.

before i knew better

reflections

1. When you pictured motherhood, before it began, what did you imagine most clearly? Was it the kind of mom you thought you'd be? What your days might look like? The connection you'd have?

_____
_____
_____
_____
_____

2. What surprised you once you were in it? What felt heavier or more beautiful than you expected?

_____
_____
_____
_____
_____

3. Where did your early expectations come from? Family? Culture? TV or social media? What you saw or didn't see growing up?

_____
_____
_____
_____
_____

anchors

These aren't goals — they are truths you may already carry.
Let these statements sit with you, as steady reminders.

I'M NOT WHO I USED TO BE . . . and that's okay.

I'M NOT LOST . . . I'm creating my path and finding my way.

I CARE DEEPLY . . . even when I'm overwhelmed.

MY LOVE . . . is more than enough.

THEIR STANDARDS AREN'T MINE . . . I define what's real for me.

MY QUIET RESILIENCE . . . is still here, every day.

I'M ALLOWED TO MAKE MISTAKES . . . this is new for me, too.

---

your thoughts, your voice

Think back to a time when you felt like you had fallen short. Was it your own expectations that shaped that feeling — or did someone else's opinions slip in? Do you still feel the same way now?

Or can you see yourself with a different kind of understanding? Give yourself grace, and write freely.

lay it down here

before i knew better

lay it down here

before i knew better

lay it down here

_____

_____

_____

_____

_____

_____

_____

_____

_____

_____

_____

_____

_____

_____

_____

_____

_____

_____

_____

_____

before i knew better

lay it down here

before i knew better

built from her armor

For most of my childhood, my mother worked 15-hour days, six days a week, in a country where she barely spoke the language. My parents owned a small business — making soups, sandwiches, and cheesesteaks that, in my opinion, put all of Philly's to shame. After their long days, they'd come home late at night, with their clothes carrying the scent of both grease and exhaustion. My mom always looked the same walking through the door, in her usual workday outfit of choice: faded jeans, a plain T-shirt, and tennis shoes.

But I'd seen the old photos. The ones tucked away inside a box on a shelf somewhere. The ones where she wore the most stylish pieces, high heels, and her long hair flowing. She looked so different in those photos. Confident. Radiant. Soft in a way I didn't yet understand.

And then there were Sundays.

Every Sunday morning before church, I'd sit on the edge of my mother's bed and watch her open her closet doors. Her focus always went to the left side, where she carefully sorted through her garment bags — as if she was opening a secret vault. She treated each piece like something sacred — like a part of herself she'd tucked away but never let go of. And when she made her choice and stepped out fully dressed, she looked like the woman I had recognized from those photos again. The woman she still was, beneath it all.

But Sundays weren't restful. They were full, just like every other day. She volunteered — sometimes because she wanted to, but often out of necessity. Because she led. Because others didn't know what to do. She cooked full meals for families and friends — never cutting corners. And somehow, she always showed up looking composed — exhaustion hidden, presence intact. For a long time, I thought she was superhuman. Strong in the kind of way that didn't flinch. Steady in the kind of way that made me feel like I didn't have the right to ever fall apart. So, I didn't. Because if my mother could do it all so gracefully, surely I could carry the weight of my own days.

It wasn't until years later, when my mother unexpectedly began to lose her vision, that something changed within me. I was certain this would give my mom enough reason to slow down — or possibly even, *break down*. Anyone else would've lost it. But not her. She was still calm. Still positive. Still showing up. I couldn't take it anymore. And instead of her, it was me who finally broke.

"Why don't you ever say it's hard? Why are you always okay? Please, just say you're tired. That this isn't fair! I see myself in so much of you, except that I'm actually exhausted. And I don't want to be strong like you anymore."

She looked at me quietly — and said nothing. Because the truth is... she was tired, too. But motherhood doesn't always leave room for softness. If she had slowed down — if she had let herself feel everything she was carrying... maybe she wouldn't have made it through. She didn't have the space to fall apart. She had to keep going. For us... *for her.*

She wasn't superhuman. She was surviving. And without even realizing it — I found myself living by that same instinct. I brought her strength into my own motherhood. Not just her grit and fight, but also her silence and self-denial.

There were plenty of days I didn't stop to see how I was doing — because that question felt like a luxury. I honestly believed that if I broke... our home would collapse. So... I held it in. And I pushed through.

Because that's what I knew.

It's taken time to sort through the things I absorbed from watching my mother — to make sense of it all, piece by piece, with more clarity than

built from her armor

resistance. To notice what shaped me over the years. Because even though so much of what she gave me was good, I've come to see there are parts I can choose to carry differently — even, lay down.

There's this strange thing that happens as I get older. A mix of understanding and some sadness when I think of my mom — not just as my mother, but as a woman. I imagine the long days that surely felt darker than she ever let on. I can see how hard she tried to make sense of a life that often asked so much of her, even as she kept showing up day after day.

I think that's why I still think about those moments we shared on Sundays. How she would step into a part of her past that felt like home — wearing pieces of her former self like armor. Reminding herself that she was still in there... *somewhere.*

And maybe that's the part I carry now, too. Not the need to be strong all the time — but the quiet belief that who I've been still matters in who I'm becoming. That softness and strength can exist side by side. That I don't have to be her to honor her. That I do get to be me.

Just me.

built from her armor

reflections

1. What did you witness growing up about how mothers showed their strength? Think of what you saw, heard, or understood about motherhood. What qualities stood out the most?

_____

_____

_____

_____

_____

2. What of that do you still carry now? Are there expectations you took on without realizing? What have you repeated? Or redefined?

_____

_____

_____

_____

_____

3. What could you say to the version of you (or your mother) — who held onto beliefs or burdens that were never hers to begin with?

_____

_____

_____

_____

_____

built from her armor

anchors

Take a moment to reflect on the words below. Notice what's been living inside you for far too long — and what you're ready to hold close now, as truth.

The message I carried:
A good mom should
never complain.
The truth I see now:
I can love my kids and
still say, "this is hard."

The message I carried:
Your kids are a true reflection
of you and your love for them.
The truth I see now:
My kids are their own people,
not my proof of worth.

The message I carried:
Keep our family
business, in the family.
The truth I see now:
Sharing my story can build
a strong circle of support.

The message I carried:
There's no time to rest —
that's lazy parenting.
The truth I see now:
Rest is not something to
be earned — it is essential.

(now, your turn)
The message I carried: _____

_____

The truth I see now: _____

_____

The message I carried: _____

_____

The truth I see now: _____

_____

built from her armor

lay it down here

built from her armor

lay it down here

_____

_____

_____

_____

_____

_____

_____

_____

_____

_____

_____

_____

_____

_____

_____

_____

_____

_____

_____

_____

_____

built from her armor

lay it down here

built from her armor

what i need, quietly

Every morning when I was little, my grandfather walked me to school. He didn't say much. I usually filled the air with nonstop chatter — the way kids do — as he smiled and listened like he understood every word. He walked beside me, holding my hand like we were in our own little world.

Then, like clockwork, about a block before we reached my school, he'd start to slow down and let go of my hand. Our conversation naturally trailing off as I'd walk ahead. And by the time I reached the school doors, he'd be just far enough behind that I could turn around, catch his eye, and wave goodbye from a distance.

I remember feeling a mix of things about that routine. I was a little girl who sometimes felt embarrassed to be walking with her grandfather while other kids were being dropped off by their parents. Part of me was relieved that he never walked me all the way to the front. But another part of me felt guilty for feeling that way at all.

It took me years to understand what my grandfather was doing all that time. Somehow, without ever having to explain, he seemed to know exactly what that little girl in me needed. He let go of my hand — not because he was tired, but to gently protect the small bits of pride I didn't even know I had yet. He watched. He noticed. And he provided — even when I didn't have the words for it then. That kind of love stays with you. It taught me what it means to be seen... and how much that matters, especially after I became a mother.

There was a time I remember in particular, telling my husband I was feeling overwhelmed. The house was a mess — dishes in the sink, laundry piling up, the kids' backpacks overflowing with unchecked papers — and emotionally, I felt just as scattered. I told him about how far behind I was on my never-ending to-do list — and through my weariness, I asked if he could sit with me for a bit.

But my husband is a doer. So instead of sitting next to me, he sprang into action. I sat on the couch, watching him move from task to task... knocking things off my list one-by-one, without hesitation. It was his way of showing up and trying to take something off my plate. His way of letting me rest. And I appreciated that. But although I knew his heart, something in me quietly ached. Because even though he was helping, he hadn't quite *heard me*.

What I needed in that moment wasn't problem-solving. It wasn't for things to get done. I just needed to feel seen. For him to sit with me in the mess — not fix it, not clean it... just be there — even for a few short minutes. Just long enough for the weight to feel a little less heavy. I could've explained it more clearly. But I didn't. Because even now, I still have a habit of minimizing what I need — of editing my asks so they don't feel like burdens.

That moment stayed with me. Because it reminded me how easy it is to silence your own needs when they're soft, or different, or hard to explain. How quickly we tell ourselves: *I should be more grateful*, instead of asking — *What do I really need right now?*

So maybe that's what I'm still learning to ask for — not louder help or bigger solutions. Just presence. The kind that doesn't rush to fix, but slows down long enough to really see me. The kind I'm also learning to offer myself, without feeling guilty about it.

Because sometimes, the hardest part isn't needing care — it's trusting that your need is reason enough. Not so someone else gets it exactly right. But so you stop editing your needs into polite suggestions — and finally say, even if it's just to yourself: *This matters to me.*

Because that's enough to matter.

reflections

1. Do you feel emotionally seen these days? Do your feelings have space to exist — without being overlooked or brushed aside?

_____

_____

_____

_____

_____

2. What would help you feel more supported now? Is it practical help, quiet understanding, or something else? List a few things that could offer you relief or comfort.

_____

_____

_____

_____

_____

3. What feels hardest about asking for support? Do you believe your needs are worth sharing? If not, why is that so?

_____

_____

_____

_____

_____

your thoughts, your voice

Think of someone you wish you could ask for support.
Or maybe you've tried, but haven't felt fully heard. Where do
you think the disconnect lies when you try to share your needs?
Beneath the words, what is your heart really asking for?

Even if it feels too hard to say out loud, try to write it here.
Let it come out as honestly as it wants to.
It's okay if they never hear these words.
You still deserve to.

what i need, quietly

lay it down here

_____

_____

_____

_____

_____

_____

_____

_____

_____

_____

_____

_____

_____

_____

_____

_____

_____

_____

_____

what i need, quietly

lay it down here

lay it down here

_____
_____
_____
_____
_____
_____
_____
_____
_____
_____
_____
_____
_____
_____
_____
_____
_____
_____
_____
_____
_____
_____

what i need, quietly

lay it down here

_____

_____

_____

_____

_____

_____

_____

_____

_____

_____

_____

_____

_____

_____

_____

_____

_____

_____

_____

what i need, quietly

returning to her

As a kid, I could read the room before anyone said a word. I knew when to step up, when to stay quiet, and how to figure things out without needing much. I led my family in small ways — translating, researching, noticing the details no one else picked up on. It wasn't something I was ever taught. In a way, I just had to do it, as many children do when the world around them moves faster than it should.

But after I became a mother, specifically after bringing my oldest son home, I found myself grasping for guidance in ways I never had before. I was no longer the one who knew what to do. Suddenly, everyone else seemed to have the answers — teachers, doctors, therapists, other moms... even strangers.

When I decided to enroll my son in daycare, I leaned hard on the advice of professionals. The director told me she had experience working with adopted children and she also had a background in psychology. I explained to her about my son's unique needs and shared my hope of finding a place that would help support and nurture him. She assured me she understood — and convinced me this was the right place for him.

But from the very first day, something felt off. He came home with a progress note — on day one. A long one. It was something minor — typical three-year-old behavior. But the way it was presented made it sound like he was already a problem. And each day after, the comments continued. What he was doing wrong. How he wasn't adjusting. What we, as his parents, should be doing differently at home.

The more I heard it, the smaller I felt. But I listened. I began to defer to their opinions. I stopped questioning the tone, the framing, the subtle judgments behind their feedback. Instead, I became a sponge. Because all of the learning and research I had done prior to adopting my son didn't seem to apply.

Even custody day caught me off guard. I was told and read so much about how traumatic it would be. We braced ourselves for an intense emotional reaction when he would leave the only life he knew. Crying, distress, even rejection — we were ready for that kind of heartbreak.

But when that time came, he wasn't fazed. Not a single tear. He said goodbye to his foster mom of two years, as casually as someone leaving a playmate at a playground. He called us *mom* and *dad* without any hesitation and held our hands like he'd always known us. None of it followed the "norm." None of it aligned with the adoption books or checklists I had studied. That's why I was so desperate. Because nothing made sense, and I didn't know what else to do. So I stopped trusting myself. And I started to disappear.

Then one afternoon, while my mom was in town visiting, she came with me to pick him up from daycare. I was nervous, as usual, unsure what new advice or critique I might hear that day. So I asked my mom to go inside and get him for me. But to my surprise, she declined. Instead, she turned to me and said, "If you're this nervous to see them... imagine how *he* must feel."

That hit me like a wave. I became so busy, listening to everyone else's opinions, that I had stopped seeing what was right in front of me: my son. And I definitely stopped listening to myself. I pulled him out of that daycare soon after. And for the first time in a long time, I felt the voice inside me come back. The one who used to lead. The one who knew how to trust what she felt. Yes, motherhood humbled me. My son made me unlearn everything I thought I ever knew. But not everything needed to be thrown away.

I had spent so much time trying to become the kind of mother the world told me I should be... that I forgot the girl who never cared to follow the norm in the first place. She was the girl who figured things out before anyone showed her how. Who trusted her gut, even when there was no map. And maybe I lost sight for a while, but I'm finding my way back.

Not by starting over — but by starting from *her*.

returning to her

reflections

1. What part of your inner voice feels most disconnected lately?
Is it your joy, your self-confidence, your clarity? When did you start
to feel this way?

_____

_____

_____

_____

_____

2. Think of a time when you felt more clear and confident in your
own instincts. What made that possible for you then?

_____

_____

_____

_____

_____

3. What feels like one small way back to her? It could be a practice,
a boundary, or simply acknowledging she's still a part of you now.

_____

_____

_____

_____

_____

anchors

Notice which statements feel familiar, like the voice you've been waiting to hear again. Sit with them. Repeat them. Believe them.

- I KNOW . . . *what feels like peace and what feels like pressure.*
- I KNOW . . . *I don't need validation to trust what I already know.*
- I KNOW . . . *when my body says "slow down."*
- I KNOW . . . *what's real — even if no one else sees it.*
- I KNOW . . . *my intuition never left — even when I doubted it.*
- I KNOW . . . *I am the expert on my child — and myself.*
- I KNOW . . . *I'm allowed to speak up, even if my voice shakes.*
- I KNOW . . . *I haven't lost my way — I'm just learning to listen again.*

(now, your turn)
- I KNOW . . . _____

your thoughts, your voice

Think of a time you didn't speak up — even when something inside you knew better. Maybe it felt easier to stay quiet. Maybe you doubted yourself, or wanted to keep the peace. What would you say now, looking back? Write freely, as a way of returning to her voice... and yours.

_____

_____

_____

_____

_____

_____

lay it down here

returning to her

lay it down here

returning to her

lay it down here

returning to her

lay it down here

---

returning to her

and she laughed again

Every now and then, I remember a story that feels random.
One that reminds me I'm still someone who laughs, who notices,
who still has stories to tell — even when they don't tie up perfectly.
This one made me laugh then. It still does now.

One night, I was aimlessly scrolling through Instagram when a familiar name popped up — *Joseph Kahn*. If you're not sure who that is, let me pause for a second to say: hello fellow Gen Xers and millennials. And yes — there was a time when people watched actual shows on MTV. One of them was *Cribs*.

Joseph Kahn is a Korean American director who had made it big. He was one of the first faces I remember seeing on TV who looked like me. He directed some of the biggest pop stars' music videos — Britney Spears, Eminem — and I'd caught him on an episode of *Cribs* many years ago. What stuck with me most? He introduced his dog with a casual, "This is *Gogi*," which in Korean means "meat." It was clearly a wink at the outdated stereotype about Koreans and dog meat — a bold, funny, self-aware moment I never forgot. It had been years since I'd thought of him, but that night, I found myself scrolling through his feed like I was catching up with an old friend.

A couple of weeks later, my husband and I went to a small, hip Korean restaurant in LA for a date night. I was happy to be out, and even happier not to be the one cooking. We were halfway through our meal when I looked up and practically dropped my spoon. A familiar face had walked in the door. It was Joseph Kahn.

He was coming toward our section, when the hostess gestured for him to sit directly next to us. He was so close that if there weren't a couple of inches between our tables, it would've looked like we were dining together. He had on a black hoodie, flip-flops... just quiet and casual. He looked exactly like I remembered from his MTV days — effortlessly cool, slightly unbothered. Like someone who didn't need anyone to know who he was... but wouldn't care if they did.

I turned to him and said, "I'm sorry... aren't you Joseph Kahn?"
He looked at me, a bit surprised, and said, "Excuse me?"
I repeated... a little less confidently, "Joseph Kahn?"
He smiled. "Yeah."
"I knew it! I remember you from MTV. On *Cribs* — you were hilarious. I cracked up when you said your dog's name was *Gogi*."
He laughed. "Yeah... I don't remember half the stuff I said on MTV."

I asked if he still directed. He shrugged and said, "Eh, I do one thing here and there." He then casually asked if we were heading to the Korean film premiere down the street. And after some continued back and forth, his friend arrived. My husband and I were finished eating by then, so we said goodbye to Joseph... and that was that.

As we were walking to the car, my husband turned to me and asked, "How do you know that guy again?" I gave him the whole story — the late-night Instagram scroll, *Cribs*, the dog. I told him how surreal it was to suddenly see him in the flesh, especially since I hadn't thought of him in years — not until he popped up on my Instagram feed. He listened intently, but then stopped and said, "Are you sure that was him?"

"What? Of course!" I replied. "We literally talked about him on MTV!"

Still... there had been a few awkward pauses in our conversation, so I understood why my husband asked. When we got in the car, I pulled out my phone — determined to prove I knew what I was talking about. I typed in "Joseph Kahn MTV Cribs." And just as quickly as I hit search, Joseph Kahn's picture appeared on my screen.

I gasped! Loudly! My husband instinctively slammed on the brakes. "What?! What happened?!" he yelled.

and she laughed again

The man I had just spent 10 minutes talking to — about directing, MTV... and even *Gogi* — was not the same person who was on my phone.

I went down an immediate rabbit hole of searches, trying to figure out where this went wrong. I searched "famous Korean Joseph MTV" and every other word combination from our conversation that I could think of. There was no way this guy could have been messing with me the whole time... right?

By the time we were almost home, I finally got a hit — a picture of the man from dinner! His name was in fact Joseph, so at least I wasn't being totally played. He was also Korean American. And also someone I had definitely seen before... just not in the way I thought.

This Joseph was Joseph Hahn — practically the same spelling, except his last name didn't start with a "K"... it started with an "H." And no, he was not a famous music video director.

Mr. *Hahn*? Well, he was a DJ... a DJ and member of Linkin Park.

Yes, as in... *that* Linkin Park. You know — the Grammy-winning, super famous band my husband had loved for years. We just had a casual conversation with one of its core members — and I spoke to him as if he was someone else entirely.

We sat in stunned silence. And then burst out laughing. We even debated turning the car around. Maybe to say thank you. But really to apologize for the most awkward exchange in the history of MTV-kind.

But we didn't. And to this day, I still wonder if that moment ever felt as strangely magical and slightly weird to him, as it did for me.

and she laughed again

a little side note

I almost didn't include this story.
It felt random — like a funny side memory that didn't quite
belong in a journal about motherhood, identity,
and holding it all together.

But then I realized: this is part of it too.
The joy. The weirdness.
The unscripted, unscheduled moments
that catch you completely off guard.

Not because they're deep — but because they aren't.
It's been years since that night, but every time I think about it,
I still smile.

And maybe that's what it reminded me of most:
it's okay to just laugh.
To hold onto the kinds of memories
that don't teach you anything or lead anywhere —
except back to yourself.

No, it wasn't a life-changing moment.
But it was one that made me feel… awake.
Like I was part of the joke — maybe even the punchline.
And honestly? That felt kind of great.

and she laughed again

your thoughts, your voice

Take a moment to remember a story.
One that made you laugh out loud or feel a little ridiculous —
in the best kind of way.
Maybe it hasn't been told in a while.
Or maybe it used to come up all the time, before life got too full.

Find it. You'll know when you do.
The one that feels like you again, even for a moment.
Write it down — just as you remember it.
No meaning or moral needed.
Just the story. Just the memories.

and she laughed again

lay it down here

_____
_____
_____
_____
_____
_____
_____
_____
_____
_____
_____
_____
_____
_____
_____
_____
_____
_____
_____

and she laughed again

lay it down here

and she laughed again

lay it down here

_____

_____

_____

_____

_____

_____

_____

_____

_____

_____

_____

_____

_____

_____

_____

_____

_____

_____

_____

_____

and she laughed again

what still fits

During COVID — when the world shut down and time felt strange — I still wore jeans. Every. Single. Day. I got dressed like I had somewhere to be, even though, like everyone else around the world, I didn't leave the house. At the time, I was a stay-at-home mom of my two kids. And getting dressed was never about vanity or trend. It was about having something that anchored me. Something that helped me mentally clock in, even if I couldn't clock out.

A few years earlier, I had made the decision to stop working after adopting our second son. There were circumstances surrounding his health that made it a non-negotiable. It was either work or him. And I chose him. But it also meant I had to find ways to remember myself in the midst of everything I was holding.

Clothes had always helped me do that. Not because I was obsessed with fashion, but because they were an extension of how I felt. The right outfit didn't make me feel prettier. It made me feel like me. And when I was wearing something that didn't match that inner sense? I felt it all day. The connection to myself through clothes was real — and as odd as it may sound, it mattered. So when that feeling started to slip away, I knew something was off.

It was after my daughter was born — our third child, and my first biological. Less than 24 hours after being discharged from giving birth, I was told to head straight to the Children's Hospital Emergency Room. What was meant to be a routine visit had turned into chaos, and I had nothing prepared — not even the basics.

Breastfeeding for the first time was its own disaster. I had no idea what I was doing. For five straight hours in a hard plastic chair, I'm pretty certain the entire emergency waiting room caught a full performance of my very own *Cirque du Soleil* — starring *The Crazy Mom Who Can't Feed Her Baby*.

I was thrown right back into motion. My husband even brought my still-packed hospital bag — the one I hadn't yet *unpacked* after coming home from delivery — straight to the new hospital, where I'd spend the next several nights. There was no time to heal or rest. Life didn't slow down after that, and over time — I felt a shift. My clothes no longer grounded me the way they used to, and eventually, I stopped getting dressed in the mornings. Not always, but more than I ever imagined. It sounds small, I know. But for me, it was unfamiliar territory. I hadn't even noticed myself letting go.

And then came my birthday. My girlfriends planned a nice dinner at a trendy restaurant to celebrate. For once, I had a reason to get dressed up again. I stood in my closet, excited to wear something — anything, that had been sitting untouched for months. But nothing felt right. The clothes weren't just uncomfortable — they didn't fit. Not just my body, but in my life anymore.

I didn't know what was in style. Were skinny jeans still a thing? Did people still do French tucks? I hadn't shopped for myself in so long, I couldn't even piece together what my style was anymore. The girl who once felt sure of herself — even in the simplest T-shirt — stood there that night, in one of the trendiest spots in West Hollywood, in head-to-toe black. Not because it was chic, but because I wanted to fade into the background.

That moment wasn't about jeans or dresses. It was about realizing how far I'd drifted from myself. The parts of me that used to show up without effort — my confidence, my instincts, my sense of self — had quietly slipped into waiting. But here's the thing: I didn't stop caring. I just stopped having the energy to pay attention. I used to know what felt like me without a second thought. Now, I look in the mirror and realize I haven't even truly looked in a long time.

Still, I'm not chasing who I used to be. I just want to be present with the woman I am today — to see her. To meet her where she is. And if that means wearing last year's jeans and breaking every fashion rule I used to know... then maybe it's not about fixing anything at all. Maybe it's about creating the space, to simply notice myself again.

what still fits

reflections

1. What small routines that once felt like everyday norms now feel like a luxury? Things like a hot shower, having time to do your hair or makeup, drinking a hot cup of coffee, exercise, etc.

_____

_____

_____

_____

_____

2. What's something that used to center you that you'd like to bring back into your life? Or maybe there's something new you want to try.

_____

_____

_____

_____

_____

3. How has your relationship with your body, energy, or well-being changed since motherhood? And what, if anything, still feels like you?

_____

_____

_____

_____

_____

an invitation

This short exercise is about honoring all the versions of you —
the ones who existed and the one still unfolding.

You can keep this list playful or reflective. It's just a small way
to notice what used to make you smile. What still feels like you —
and what you're ready to release or reclaim.

then:

THE PERFUME *I wore:*

THE SONG *I loved:*

MY GO-TO OUTFIT *that felt like me:*

A HOBBY or RITUAL *that grounded me:*

A PHRASE or MINDSET *I lived by:*

now:

A SCENT *I love:*

A SONG THAT *speaks to me:*

WHAT I FEEL *best wearing:*

A HABIT or RITUAL *that helps me feel present:*

A PHRASE or MINDSET *that anchors me:*

what still fits

lay it down here

_____

_____

_____

_____

_____

_____

_____

_____

_____

_____

_____

_____

_____

_____

_____

_____

_____

_____

_____

_____

what still fits

lay it down here

_____

_____

_____

_____

_____

_____

_____

_____

_____

_____

_____

_____

_____

_____

_____

_____

_____

_____

_____

_____

what still fits

lay it down here

_____

_____

_____

_____

_____

_____

_____

_____

_____

_____

_____

_____

_____

_____

_____

_____

_____

_____

_____

_____

what still fits

lay it down here

_____
_____
_____
_____
_____
_____
_____
_____
_____
_____
_____
_____
_____
_____
_____
_____
_____
_____
_____
_____
_____

what still fits

i would never

I used to have this long, running list in my head of all the things I swore I'd never do as a mom. Very minimal use of iPads, if at all. Fast food only on occasion. Toys would never overflow in the house. My car would stay clean. And no minivan. Absolutely no minivan.

But of course, as it always seems to go — the list started slipping before I could even keep track of it.

Aside from my oldest son's colorful vocabulary when we first became a family, there was another word he'd say — less dramatic, but just as perplexing: *mekdonku*. My husband and I both speak Korean and English, but the word wasn't from either language. He said it often enough that we knew it wasn't just random toddler talk. It became this little mystery that followed us around.

And then one day, it clicked — as we passed the giant golden arches, driving in the car. *Mekdonku* was my son's way of saying *McDonald's*. He had been recognizing it every time he saw one. And once we finally put two and two together, I noticed his eyes light up — like he was seeing an old friend. It was his own little pathway to comfort.

In a life that felt foreign and new, that red and yellow sign was familiar to him. And so, as I crossed "no fast food" off my list of things I once promised myself I'd never do... I have to admit — it became a bit of a saving grace for us, too.

The truth is, there are so many things that divide us as moms. Stay-at-home moms versus working moms. Breastfeeding versus formula. Co-sleeping versus sleep-training. And it just keeps getting worse — down to the type of toothpaste our kids use. Anything and everything has a side. Even when we're not trying to judge one another, the comparisons find a way in. And every choice we make feels like a silent vote cast in an invisible, endless debate.

Over the years, I joined countless parenting groups to help me navigate motherhood: anything adoption-related groups, Korean adoption groups, domestic adoption groups, special needs mom groups, trauma-informed parenting circles, medical needs communities.

You name it... *I'm probably in it.*

But the crazy thing is, even within these safe spaces — among moms who share similar journeys — there are still so many divides. And sometimes, they're even louder. Because everyone seems to have an opinion, or know exactly what they're talking about — since they've "been there too." So then, you end up questioning yourself all over again.

My head would feel like it was spinning out of control whenever I'd get a notification of another new post or comment. So much so that I had to ignore them completely. What I thought would be places of genuine support ended up doing the exact opposite. And that's when it really sank in for me: no one should ever have the right to judge you or your parenting. Ever.

Because no one else is raising your child. No one else has walked through your exact story, or understands the intricate details of your family. Even with both of my boys — on paper, their stories are practically identical. Both are adopted. Both of Korean descent. Both with traumas and specific needs. You'd think I'd be a pro by now. But the reality is, I'm actually far from it. Their needs and personalities are so vastly different that I can barely keep up most days.

What I've learned — and what I want to remember — is that our motherhood journeys are never meant to look the same. Not even when they're under the same roof. The best thing we can do for each other is to build each other up in community and release the pressure to do it any other way but yours.

At the end of the day, it doesn't matter how you got here. What really matters is that *you're here*. And you're doing it — in the way that only you can.

i would never

You're showing up, even on the days it feels impossible. You're learning and loving in ways that no one else will ever fully see. And whether or not anyone says it out loud — it counts. It all counts.

END OF STORY.

.

.

.

Okay... it's not really the end, but it would've sounded so powerful to close it right there in **BIG, BOLD LETTERS.**

Here's the thing. Even though I believe with everything in me that no one has the right to judge you, that doesn't always drown out the self-doubt or shame we sometimes carry. Even when we know better, we still question whether we're doing enough.

The truth is, we are all still students in this motherhood journey. We're continuously learning and going to get it wrong from time to time. So as much as I want to tell you to *mekdonku* all the haters out there — *(oops... I meant the other word he actually said)* — I'll just say this instead: you're not alone if you still second-guess yourself in this parenting thing.

I'm a member of that club too.

i would never

reflections

1. What is something you once swore you'd never do as a parent that you now see differently? How did that shift happen? What did it teach you about giving yourself permission to change?

_____

_____

_____

_____

_____

2. Do you ever feel judged for how you parent? How has it affected the choices you make or how you see yourself as a mother?

_____

_____

_____

_____

_____

3. Has your perspective toward other parents changed over time? Do you have more or less empathy for different parenting styles?

_____

_____

_____

_____

_____

your thoughts, your voice

Think of a moment when you felt judged as a mother. Maybe it was a passing comment, or something that stayed with you longer than you expected. What did it feel like in your body and your heart?

Now, widen the lens a bit. Imagine another mother carrying that same weight — possibly more often than others. What do you hope she knows deep down? How might the way you see her, or the way you respond, help to ease some of what she's holding inside?

Write to yourself first, as you would to a friend: with the kindness and reassurance you deserved in that moment. Then, let your words reach her too — the mother you don't know, but who has felt that same sting of judgment.

And if no one has said it to either of you lately, let me be the one to say it here: You're a good mom. And you're not alone in this.

i would never

lay it down here

_____

_____

_____

_____

_____

_____

_____

_____

_____

_____

_____

_____

_____

_____

_____

_____

_____

_____

_____

i would never

lay it down here

i would never

lay it down here

i would never

before you turn the page...

You've just spent time listening inward —
maybe more honestly than you have in a while.

You've remembered what it was like before you knew better,
what you carried in, what you've needed quietly,
and the parts of you that still feel worth returning to.

You've asked yourself what still fits — not just on the outside,
but in the way you move through your life now.
And slowly, you've made room for the woman you are right here.

Not the one trying to do it all.
But the one who's learning to stay with herself —
with care, honesty, and connection.

You don't have to go back to who you were.
You're allowed to grow forward in a way that
honors every version you've ever been.

Sit with that for a bit.
And then, when you're ready... *let's keep going.*

part ii: the life you hold close

→

exploring the invisible weight, emotional labor, and quiet courage of who you are today

holding it all together

There's a version of you that looks like she's got it together. Maybe not thriving, maybe not rested — but still getting it all done. The lunches. The fallouts. The appointments. The laundry. The everything. That was me for a long time. Just moving — on autopilot, in motion, doing what needed to be done.

When I became a mom, it wasn't gradual. There was no easing in. We went from zero to a hundred — adopting two sons within six months, then giving birth to a third — all in a few whirlwind years. I was managing. At first, surprisingly well, given everything. Not exactly "Mom of the Year," but not falling apart either. And for a while, that felt like enough. I told myself: *This is just what motherhood is.* Chaos. Stretched capacity. Learning how to keep going anyway.

But about a year ago, I hit a wall I didn't see coming. Literally. We were sitting at a red light, on the way to pick up our oldest son from soccer practice. That's when an SUV coming from the other direction hit us head-on at full speed. It was jarring, yes — but it was also the moment I felt the ground drop out from under me. As soon as the car stopped moving, it hit me — not just the physical pain, but the sharp awareness of how fragile it all was. I could have left my children without a mother. And for the first time, I understood that no amount of planning, multitasking, or managing could protect them — or me.

From that day on, I wasn't just holding everyday life. I was holding my kids' traumas. My own recovery. My husband's pain. I was fielding new waves of anxiety in my son, who couldn't bear to let me out of his sight. My daughter had meltdown after meltdown anytime she had to get in a car. I was healing physically, but mentally, I was unraveling. And the hardest part was — I couldn't stop it.

I was no longer "holding it all together."
I was holding on by a thread.

I could feel myself slipping. But in my mind, I kept telling myself to *get it together*. I didn't have time to feel sorry for myself. Depression and anxiety would just add another layer of things I didn't have the energy to deal with. Out of desperation, I reached out to my doctor for help — but the medications left me with more side effects than relief. Nothing seemed to land. So I did the only thing I knew how to do. I took it upon myself to fix it. And at that time... that meant shutting everything else out of my life.

I stopped making or returning calls. I stopped checking in with friends... and myself. I was using what little energy I had left in my emergency reserve and rationing it out for my family's needs. I was in hyper-numb overdrive. I was surviving. And still — I showed up. *Because moms do.*

But eventually, my body kept sounding alarms — through fatigue, migraines, hair loss, and a creeping sense of disconnection I couldn't shake. I finally opened up to a friend over the phone. It was hard to do, but after I did, something in me softened. The weight didn't go away, but it lifted slightly — just enough for me to breathe again.

And a few weeks later, I started writing. Quietly. Privately. Not because I had answers, but because I needed a place to finally put the pieces down. That was actually the moment this journal began. It became my place to *not* hold it all together. To fall apart a little. To ask myself the questions I was afraid to answer. To name what I was really carrying — without feeling like I shouldn't.

If you're holding this journal, I can only imagine you're holding on to a lot, too. The invisible weight. The slow unraveling. The exhaustion of keeping it going for everyone else. So take these pages and use them how you need. To name the things you're avoiding inside. To tell the truth about what it's costing you. To say: *I'm tired. I need help.* Or *I'm here — but I'm worn out.*

You don't have to be the strong one right now.
Just be the real one. She's worth knowing too.

holding it all together

reflections

1. Is there something you've been managing so well (or not so well), that you haven't let yourself admit how heavy it's been? Do tasks automatically fall on you, without ever any discussion?

_____

_____

_____

_____

_____

2. Have you noticed any signs — whether physical or emotional — that you're moving beyond what feels sustainable these days?

_____

_____

_____

_____

_____

3. What would it feel like to ask for help, without guilt or hesitation? If that feels hard, ask yourself why. What fears are holding you back?

_____

_____

_____

_____

_____

anchors

Before you move on, take a moment to read these words for what they really are — not answers, but reminders. You've been holding a lot. You don't have to sort through it all right now. Let this be a small place to land before you keep going.

My worth is not measured by how much I can or can't do.

I can put something down, without failing anyone.

Letting myself feel is not the same as letting everything go.

Even if my hands are full, **I still deserve time for me**.

The world won't fall apart if I pause — **but I might if I don't**.

---

your thoughts, your voice

Think about what you've been holding, maybe longer than you even realized. What has it taken out of you to keep going like this? What have you been carrying quietly, hoping no one would notice?

Use this space to name what's been too much, or what's felt hard to admit out loud. You don't need to solve it here. Just give it somewhere to land. Even for a moment, let it rest outside of you.

lay it down here

lay it down here

lay it down here

holding it all together

lay it down here

---

holding it all together

tend to her, too

Whenever a friend asks if I'm taking time for "self-care,"
I honestly have to stop and think about how to answer.

We hear the word self-care a lot. It usually sounds like spa days,
wine nights, weekend getaways. All wonderful — yes.
But for some moms, myself included, they're not always realistic.

And when they're out of reach, we're left wondering if we're
neglecting ourselves... or yet again, failing at something else.

But real self-care isn't always big. Or photo-worthy.
It can be a whisper. A small pause.
A moment where you say, *I'm still here.*

Let this next page be a soft place to return to.
A list of little things that can offer you a breath or warmth.
Pick one. Pick ten. Pick the entire list.
Or simply sit with the idea that you're allowed to
do something... *for you.*

That alone is care.

This isn't another list of things you need to complete.
There's no prize for doing it all.

But this is a list of permissions.
Of quiet invitations.
Of reminders that you need time for you, too.

a list of permissions

Small ways to show your<u>self care</u> — the kind that remembers you, too.
Check them off as you go, or simply return whenever you need.

your body

○ make that special appointment you've been putting off (hair, nails, etc.)
○ schedule your annual doctor's appointment (yours, not someone else's)
○ buy a sample-sized (or full-sized) product you've been eyeing
○ put on something that brings your mood up, even if you're staying in
○ don't change out of your pajamas or sweats all day — intentionally
○ scream the stress away into a pillow, into the air, out of your body
○ do a quick 10 minute stretch, dance or exercise video
○ add your own: _____

your mind

○ cancel or reschedule one thing that feels heavy right now
○ re-read a favorite book — or just a page — because it speaks to you
○ allow yourself to just sit and be in silence for 15 minutes (no phone)
○ do a 5-minute meditation (bonus points if you light a candle)
○ take a selfie, just to remember you were here — present and beautiful
○ say "no" to something that's bringing in stress — without over-explaining
○ step outside for 10 minutes — relax, be present, take intentional breaths
○ add your own: _____

your heart

○ listen to a favorite, feel-good song from a decade (or two) ago
○ call someone you've been thinking about, just to say hi
○ watch a show or movie you've been putting off (a series is even better!)
○ order food from the place you're craving — not where others want to eat
○ write 1 or 2 things you are proud of, appreciate, or love about yourself
○ pray, journal, or say out loud the words you need to hear most today
○ add your own: _____

tend to her, too

lay it down here

tend to her, too

lay it down here

_____

_____

_____

_____

_____

_____

_____

_____

_____

_____

_____

_____

_____

_____

_____

_____

_____

_____

_____

_____

_____

tend to her, too

the invisible load

A couple of years ago, we unexpectedly moved into our current home after hitting wall after wall with my middle child's school district. We tried everything we could to help him transition into public school — meetings, plans, patience, hope. But the system wasn't built for kids like him... and it showed.

Eventually, I found a district that actually listened. They understood what we were asking for our son. So we made the tough but necessary decision to move. We uprooted, almost immediately. And both of my boys started at their new school after their peers had already begun.

We stood out — new faces in an already-connected community. I'd wait at pickup, learning names, smiling politely, trying to remember who I'd already met. Slowly, those everyday interactions turned into something warmer. Quick *hellos* became conversations. And conversations turned into invitations.

Lots of invitations.

Playdates. Park meet-ups. Little "let's hang after school" gestures that were extremely kind and thoughtful. But if I'm being totally honest... they were also exhausting. Because as much as I wanted to say yes, every invitation felt a lot heavier than it should have.

Of course I didn't want to be the mom who always said no. I truly liked some of these women. I wanted my son to have that extra time with his classmates. To make friends and feel more comfortable in his new surroundings.

But behind every casual plan was a cascade of decisions — quiet calculations I couldn't explain in passing. And after turning down more invitations than I could count... I knew I couldn't keep holding them off forever. I told my husband, "I think I need to go to at least one, just so I don't look like the anti-social mom who doesn't care."

So I did. And it was fine. It was nice, even — for a moment.

Because when we got home — I was reminded of what these outings cost us. Not just the energy, but the ways they stirred something deeper — for my son... and for me.

What others don't see is how hard transitions are for my son. How even the mention of a new plan can trigger an emotional spiral. How something as casual as a playdate requires a mental load most people never have to consider.

They don't see how much lives beneath a simple "yes." Or the part of me that wishes it were easy to fit in — when in reality, it takes maximum effort just to meet the baseline. They don't know that I haven't slept through the night in eight years — because of my son's intense anxiety and the quiet ways I care for him in the dark. The constant research I do to help my kids navigate their needs. The doctors and therapists I speak with, more than my own friends.

And honestly? When I do manage to show up somewhere — on time, with a little energy, maybe even with makeup on — I hate being praised for it. Because no one knows what it's costing me.

It's not the things I don't do.
It's the weight behind everything I do.

the invisible load

reflections

1. What does it take for you to show up — in everything that you do? The stress, the exhaustion, the managing... what do people miss when they see you doing it all so "effortlessly?"

_____

_____

_____

_____

_____

2. What responsibilities, worries, or anxieties take up constant space in your mind — even if they may go unnoticed by others?

_____

_____

_____

_____

_____

3. What's one way you've felt misunderstood lately? What do people assume... and what's the truth you wish they knew?

_____

_____

_____

_____

_____

_____

the invisible load

your thoughts, your voice

You've likely had moments where you held your tongue.
Times when someone made a comment or assumption —
and you let it go, because explaining would've taken too much
out of you. Maybe you told yourself it wasn't worth your energy.
Or maybe you cried when no one was watching.

If you could say what you were really feeling to that person —
to the friend, the teacher, the stranger — what would it be?
Let this be a space where you don't have to be gracious or polite.
You can be honest. Protective. Direct. Angry.
Say what you needed to say —
without shrinking it down to make others more comfortable.
Not for their understanding, but for your own release.

And when you're done, let it go — gracefully... *or with fire.*
Because their judgments don't deserve any space in your story.

lay it down here

_____

_____

_____

_____

_____

_____

_____

_____

_____

_____

_____

_____

_____

_____

_____

_____

_____

_____

_____

_____

_____

lay it down here

_____
_____
_____
_____
_____
_____
_____
_____
_____
_____
_____
_____
_____
_____
_____
_____
_____
_____
_____
_____
_____
_____

lay it down here

_____

_____

_____

_____

_____

_____

_____

_____

_____

_____

_____

_____

_____

_____

_____

_____

_____

_____

_____

_____

_____

the invisible load

lay it down here

the invisible load

the life i didn't choose

It was before we had kids. We were still young, full of dreams, mapping out what our future might look like. I had just been offered a position on the other side of the country — the kind I had always wanted. A role I imagined would anchor my career, build momentum, and lead to something fulfilling. To something bigger. To success.

It was the dream.

But around the same time, my mom's health was on the decline. And without hesitation, I chose to stay close. To help. To be present. To be the daughter I knew she needed.

I told myself it was the right decision — and it was. But that didn't mean it was easy. There was a part of me that felt like I was always the one putting my own life on pause.

I could never fully blame my mom — it was my choice to stay. But I did feel the quiet grief of what I was letting go. The slow ache of always being the dependable one. The one who adjusted. Who stayed. Who pressed pause on her own life while everyone else got to move forward.

A couple years passed by and fortunately, my mom was getting better. With my mother needing less and less help, I eventually went back to work and took on a different job. But even as our lives seemed to settle down, my husband and I realized we still had a yearning to move to California. So, I asked my boss for a transfer to our West Coast office. And within weeks, we packed up our lives and moved across the country.

On my first day walking into my new office building — after all the meetings and introductions — I finally had a minute to relax. I sat at my desk and wondered what this new chapter might bring. It felt like a fresh start. A healing, in its own way. A moment that was finally... mine. I stared out the window, just taking in the incredible view.

And that's when I saw it.

Of all the places in California our West Coast office could've been — it was directly across the street from the building where I had once turned down my dream job. The one I thought about so often over the years. And now, I had a clear view of it... whether I liked it or not.

Each morning, as I drank my coffee at work, I'd find myself staring out the window — wondering what it would have been like if I had said yes instead. How close I was now to the life I once thought I wanted. So close I could almost touch it... and yet, so far from the version of me who once dreamed it.

It wasn't regret. It was something else.

A bittersweet awareness of how our path reroutes us — and how sometimes, the choices we make out of love or necessity don't lead to the life we imagined... but to the one that shapes us in other ways.

I still think about that life sometimes. The one where I took the leap. Moved forward. Chased something different. But I've come to let go of that part of me I thought I once knew — and focus instead on living where I'm at. With presence, and meaning. Because the things I once thought mattered most... feel distant now — like they belonged to someone else entirely.

And for all I know, if I had taken that job...
that same person might be drinking her coffee every morning at work,
staring out the window at my building —
wondering what her life would've been like...
... if she had stayed.

the life i didn't choose

reflections

After sharing this story, I wanted to continue the conversation in a different way. Because this part — the life we didn't choose — often holds more than we say out loud. We all have versions of ourselves we once imagined. The job you almost took. The move you talked yourself out of. The relationship you walked away from. The dream you paused, thinking it was just for a short while.

Maybe it wasn't even a clear moment — just a slow drift away from the life you thought might be yours. And while you may not regret the path you're on, there are times you still wonder:
What would've happened if I had said yes instead of no?
Would I feel more fulfilled? More like myself? More free?

These questions don't always come up when life is going well. They tend to surface in the quiet, tired moments — when your mind wanders to a side of you that didn't end up... *here.*

But what if that wondering isn't really about that life at all? What if it's less about the life you turned away from — and more about something inside you, still asking to be heard? That's what this is for. To bring forward what's been left behind. To let yourself feel whatever comes with it — without shame or rushing to make sense of it. And if you're willing, take a moment to imagine that other version of you, too. The one who said yes to the thing you said no. She just might be wondering about your life, here today.

Because the grass isn't always greener... it's just green.
And all the what if's in the world can't ever replace *what is.*

So, my dear friend — it's time.
Not to chase something new... but to notice what's already here.
And in that noticing, I hope something inside you finally exhales.
Not because this is where you have to stay.
But because now... you get to choose where you'll go next.

the life i didn't choose

your thoughts, your voice

Take a moment to turn inward — to notice what feelings are rising. It might be a thought about the path you didn't take. Or a deeper meaning you've discovered in the one you did. Whatever surfaces — regret, hope, wonder, sadness, gratitude — write it down.

What have you left behind? What still matters?
What do you want now — even if, especially if — it's different from what you once imagined? Let it come freely, just as it is.

lay it down here

---

the life i didn't choose

lay it down here

the life i didn't choose

lay it down here

the life i didn't choose

lay it down here

the life i didn't choose

still learning to receive

I remember the day I became a mother of two. It was a whirlwind. We had never planned to adopt again — especially not just six months after bringing home our oldest son. But our social worker reached out with a call we didn't expect. She told us about a baby boy who had already been through so much. She said, "I had to ask you. You just feel like the right parents for him."

We said yes on a Friday. Her response: "Wonderful! You can bring him home on Sunday." I was in shock. Our first adoption took two years — now, we had two days. And unlike before, we had nothing ready. Especially not for a baby, when our oldest son had come home to us as a toddler.

But in the midst of the chaos, something unexpected happened: our community showed up. Word spread, and donations poured into our home within a day. Car seats. Strollers. Baby clothes. Bottles. Formula. Things I hadn't even had time to think about were suddenly on my doorstep. It was overwhelming, in the best way — but also hard to find myself accepting so much help from others.

The idea of receiving help wasn't something I was used to. I was always the self-sufficient one — the one who preferred giving support rather than receiving it. So being on this side of things felt really uncomfortable. But I embraced it... because I had to. There was no time to second-guess, especially with a baby on the way. But mentally, that was about as far as I was willing to go. I was willing to let our community help with stuff. Just not with *me*.

The true unraveling happened after we brought our son home. He had already spent three months in the NICU and undergone multiple surgeries. So on that first day, the one thing I knew I had to prioritize was picking up his medications. And once my brand new baby finally went down for a nap, I told my husband I would gladly run out to the pharmacy. Because truthfully, my mind was still playing catch-up... and I needed a minute to breathe.

I had just become a sudden mom of two, and I hadn't had time to process any of it. So when I saw a line at the pharmacy drive-thru, I never felt more relieved in my life. Those few extra minutes to myself — to decompress — felt like a spa day. But when it was my turn to pull up to the window, the pharmacist brought me back to reality real quick. My son's paperwork hadn't been filed. He wasn't insured. And the out-of-pocket costs were staggering.

I sat in my car, crying. Defeated. I kept wondering: *what did I get myself into?* That's when I got a text from one of the moms who had been helping us — just checking in. I hesitantly told her what was going on with the pharmacy. She responded immediately. Her husband was a doctor, and before I could reply back — she said they'd be right over, to help however they could.

I thought I had time — just a few more minutes to sit with my emotions and then collect myself. But when I walked into the house, to my surprise... they were already there. Meeting my boys. Chatting with my husband. I stood there — dazed and puffy-eyed. As I tried to pull myself together, I spotted my bra — flung across the couch like an elephant in the room no one wanted to acknowledge. I had thrown it off just before running out the door, because my heart felt like it was pounding out of my chest. The irony? *Now it actually was.*

My husband, clearly hadn't even noticed, so I was on my own in trying to hide it. I side-stepped over to the sofa, and tried tossing it behind a pillow. But instead of falling behind it — my bra landed on top of it, front and center. Spotlighted for all to see.

In that moment, I gave up. And... I gave in.

I broke down and let it all out — all of the emotions I'd been trying so hard to hold in came crashing down. That was a turning point for me. I stopped pretending that everything was okay and started opening up to some women who in turn, became incredible friends. From that moment on, they didn't just

still learning to receive

drop things off at the door. They sat with me. Checked in. Prayed over us. Loved us in a way that felt genuine. Not the type of kindness done out of politeness or pity — but the kind that meets you fully when you put down the facade. It was a lot to take in — but it was also, incredibly healing.

It didn't come naturally. I still felt awkward, and of course, guilty for constantly being on the receiving end of these friendships. But I kept being reminded — sometimes out loud, sometimes through quiet presence — that it was okay to let people in. That I didn't have to earn help. That receiving was part of being in community.

And over time, I learned that expressing my genuine gratitude was also a form of giving. That vulnerability and appreciation could exist in the same breath. That being poured into, when you're running dry, can be the most honest kind of friendship there is.

Seasons change constantly. There are times when I've had more to give. And times when I've had nothing left. But I've come to know — friendship isn't a tally. It's not about keeping score. It's about the courage to offer love and to receive it. Even when it's uncomfortable. Even when you feel undeserving...

... especially then.

reflections

1. When support is offered to you — what comes up? Do you lean in? Hesitate? Feel indebted, guilty, or unsure how to accept it?

2. What have you believed you needed to do — or had to be — in order to be cared for? Where did these beliefs come from?

3. Have you been more of a giver or receiver lately? We're always both, but what's been louder in this season. Has it made you feel more connected or disconnected with others?

an invitation

Sometimes the hardest part of receiving is feeling as if we are
a burden. But what if we tried changing our thoughts —
from feelings of guilt... to gratitude?

It may take some time to make that shift. But try to remind
yourself: you are worthy of care. Let love in without apology.
So let's start here. Because practice makes progress.

- *Instead of* . . . "I'm sorry I haven't been myself lately."
  - **» Try** . . . "Thank you for loving me, even in the messy moments."

- *Instead of* . . . "I'm sorry I had to cancel our plans again."
  - **» Try** . . . "Thank you for understanding I'm juggling a lot right now."

- *Instead of* . . . "I'm sorry I keep circling back to the same struggles."
  - **» Try** . . . "Thank you for being there for me while I work through this."

- *Instead of* . . . "I'm sorry I've been so hard to reach lately."
  - **» Try** . . . "Thank you for checking in, even when I feel so far away."

(now, your turn)

- *Instead of* . . . _____
  - **» Try** . . . _____

- *Instead of* . . . _____
  - **» Try** . . . _____

"Even when you feel emptied, you are still worthy of being filled."

your thoughts, your voice

Think of someone you've been wanting to reach out to, but haven't yet. Maybe it's an old friend you miss. Or someone you see often, but you haven't quite moved past the "cordial acquaintance" stage.

What would it feel like to invite them in — not with heaviness, but with honesty? Even if it's as simple as a cup of coffee, if that's what you truly want... why not ask? Connection doesn't have to be deep to be real — but it does need to be genuine.

And if what you're craving is a conversation that goes a bit deeper... what's been holding you back from taking that step?

It's easy to let friendships slip into the background as we get older. And while we may not always know where to begin, we still long for closeness — even if we don't always say it out loud.

Take this time to ask yourself: what kind of connection do I hope for — or maybe even need right now?
Be honest. Be specific. Be vulnerable.
And maybe — when it feels right — share a little of your heart with the person who came to mind.

still learning to receive

lay it down here

still learning to receive

lay it down here

_____

still learning to receive

lay it down here

_____
_____
_____
_____
_____
_____
_____
_____
_____
_____
_____
_____
_____
_____
_____
_____
_____
_____
_____
_____
_____

still learning to receive

lay it down here

From someone still learning to receive, too...
Thank you for making space for connection —
between two people figuring this out as we go.

In a quiet, unexpected way, *you've given me*
the courage to share more than I thought I could.

But now, it's your turn to be on the receiving end
of that same grace. Let it reach you. It's time.

halfway, fully together

In 2020, I ran my first — and only — half marathon. I'm not an avid runner. I don't even like running. In fact, I hate it. But I always loved the idea of it — the thought of a runner's high, of releasing stress while moving forward, one step at a time. A half marathon had been on my bucket list since I was a teenager. And decades later, three years into motherhood, I finally did it.

Motherhood, for me, has ebbed and flowed between crazy, crazier, and just plain insane. I think I started training somewhere between crazier and insane. It wasn't exactly planned, but it started when I would push my boys to the park in a double stroller — walking at first, then slowly jogging home. Sometimes, sprinting home because one of them would inevitably remember they needed to use the bathroom, even though they swore they didn't just minutes before.

Eventually, that turned into a routine. And somewhere along the way, the idea of running a half crept back into my mind. I wasn't fast, but let's be honest: at that point in my life, speed wasn't exactly the goal. It kept my energetic boys somewhat contained for a few minutes and gave me the tiniest pocket of time where I felt like I was doing something for me. Even if I still hated every step.

After a couple of months in this routine, I thought: *Why not? It's now or never.* So, I signed up for an official race. I didn't care about my personal time. Even if I walked across the finish line, at least I could finally cross it off my list.

Race day arrived, and I felt anxious and nervous — but mostly, I felt happy. I had signed up for me. No one else. Just me. And it felt so good to be alone for once. Really alone. Not the kind of alone where you tell yourself it counts as "me time" while you're rushing through the grocery store. This was thirteen point one miles of alone — and in its own strange way, it felt like a way back to myself again.

Even though I still hated running, I felt good out there. Better than I ever expected. For the first time in what felt like forever, I could actually hear my own thoughts — no snack requests, no refereeing arguments from the stroller, no background noise. Just the sound of my own breath as I took each step. That and the slow, '90s R&B music playing in my ears. (Not everyone's top choice to get your adrenaline pumping, I know — but this was my happy place.)

I thought about my kids. My marriage. Myself. I actually felt really proud of the life I was living, as a film reel was streaming through my mind. The grief, the gratitude... everything started to feel like an emotional high. Or — *was it... a runner's high?* The one I never fully believed existed but hoped it did. There it was, creeping in and I was finally crossing into it.

But then... *I ate it.*

At mile eleven, I tripped over my own two feet and landed flat on my face. (Which felt pretty on-brand at that point.) I wasn't even embarrassed. I was pissed. I lost all my momentum, my rhythm, and whatever determination I had left. But as cliché as it sounds... I got up — and you guessed it — I kept going.

The last two miles after that were brutal. It felt like I was starting from zero all over again. I was running on the lowest low. My energy drained, my body aching, and my mind was clouded with thoughts of giving up — when I caught sight of my husband and kids near the finish line. They were cheering, beaming with pride — not knowing I'd been crying minutes earlier, feeling like I had failed even at this. But it didn't matter to them. They didn't care about what happened. To them, the *only* thing that mattered was that I was there. Just there.

I still hate running to this day. But in a way, that race was the perfect metaphor for motherhood: the hard work, the little wins, the inevitable wipeouts, the moments of reflection — and the reminder that, in the end, it's not about how gracefully you ran. It's that you showed up. That you loved. That you were loved. That you kept going. Through it all — toward what mattered most.

halfway, fully together

reflections

1. Can you think of a moment — big or small — where you showed up with care and effort, but still walked away feeling like it just didn't go the way you imagined?

_____

_____

_____

_____

2. Do you give yourself enough credit for your progress — or do you find yourself replaying the things that didn't go so well?

_____

_____

_____

_____

3. When self-doubt creeps in, what might help you see things with a little more kindness — or a more balanced perspective?

_____

_____

_____

_____

an invitation

We're often our own harshest critics. But what if you saw yourself through the eyes of the people who love you most? Take a moment to consider how they might see things differently in you. Look at the words below for some inspiration. Then, write with kindness.

resilience	care	presence	warmth
showing up	patience	quiet strength	love
dedication	grace	courage	truth

Even when I look or feel like a mess, they might see . . .

_____

When I feel I could've done something better, they might see . . .

_____

When I make mistakes or show my flaws, they might see . . .

_____

When I'm barely getting through the day, they might see . . .

_____

Even in the smallest, everyday moments, they might feel . . .

_____

anchors

Out of every mom I've ever known who questions whether she's doing enough — two things always connect us:
The fear that we're falling short.
And the unwavering love we have for our children.

And that's the thing about good moms. We don't worry because we're failing. We worry because we care — deeply.
And that alone says everything.
We're not perfect — not even close.
But our children aren't asking for perfect.
They're just asking for _us_.
And they love us still. What a gift that is.

halfway, fully together

lay it down here

halfway, fully together

lay it down here

_____

halfway, fully together

lay it down here

halfway, fully together

lay it down here

---

halfway, fully together

the most important story

You've followed my words through these pages.
But now — let this last story be yours, fully.
Not prompted or polished.
Just real. Just yours.

You don't have to explain, justify, or make it make sense.
You get to start this page however you wish.
With a truth. A memory. A release. A hope.

A whisper of what you need.
A declaration of what you deserve.

Because your voice is worth hearing... especially by you.
You just needed a place to begin.

lay it down here

---

the most important story

lay it down here

_____

_____

_____

_____

_____

_____

_____

_____

_____

_____

_____

_____

_____

_____

_____

_____

_____

_____

_____

_____

the most important story

lay it down here

the most important story

lay it down here

the most important story

lay it down here

_____

_____

_____

_____

_____

_____

_____

_____

_____

_____

_____

_____

_____

_____

_____

_____

_____

_____

_____

_____

the most important story

if this is where we pause

I hope something in this journal reminded you that you're not alone. That your exhaustion has a reason. That your love has depth. And that your story still matters. Maybe you didn't fill in every section, or you wrote more than you ever expected. However you showed up was exactly how it should be.

And if you're still holding more than you know how to say, I hope you keep this journal close. Not because you need to finish it, but because you're worthy of a space that holds you — without asking you to be anything more than you already are.

I've held these stories close for years, not knowing if they'd ever matter to anyone but me. But I hope they met you in some small way. Writing them helped me make sense of the parts of motherhood that truly caught me off guard. I never imagined that a title so beautifully humbling as "mom" could carry this undercurrent of loneliness — even when you're surrounded by the people you love.

And I think that might be where the disconnect has been all along: the mask we feel like we have to wear, because we assume no one else is feeling this way. But the truth is, we're not the only ones. We never were. And when we stop hiding that, we get to make room for others to do the same.

As strange as it sounds, sharing this with you helped me feel a little more connected to something real. And I hope that being here helped you feel the same. As if you can open up a little more too, in your own way, in your own time. Because you deserve to be met with the same care you've given to me, just by choosing to be here. I'm so grateful to have met you through these pages. Thank you for showing up. Thank you for sharing your heart.

Thank you for *meeting me here.*

meet me here

www.ingramcontent.com/pod-product-compliance
Lightning Source LLC
Chambersburg PA
CBHW041537120626
46551CB00019B/2738